EXPLORING

Landmarks

Villages

Danielle Sensier and Amanda Earl

WAYLAND

Landmarks

Exploring Inner Cities

Exploring Seaside Towns

Exploring Suburbs

Exploring Villages

Cover: The picturesque village of Gunnerside, set in the hills of North Yorkshire (main picture); making silage in County Down, Northern Ireland (top); and a boy on a bike ride in South Wales (left).
Title page: Bodinnick fishing village, in Cornwall.
Contents page: A children's farm.

For Mimi-rose Isabella.

Series editor: Katie Orchard
Designers: Tim Mayer/Mark Whitchurch
Production controller: Carol Stevens

First published in 1997 by Wayland Publishers Limited
61 Western Road, Hove
East Sussex, BN3 1JD, England

British Library Cataloguing in Publication Data
Sensier, Danielle
    Exploring Villages. – (Landmarks)
    1. Villages – juvenile literature
    I. Title II. Earl, Amanda
    307.7'2

ISBN 0 7502 1884 3

Typeset by Mayer Media/Mark Whitchurch
Printed and bound in Italy by G. Canale S.p.A.

Picture acknowledgements:
CEPHAS Frank B. Higham 11 (left), Frank B. Higham 26 (bottom); James Davis Travel Photography **cover**, 5 (top);East Sussex County Council 7 (bottom right), 43; Eye Ubiquitous **cover** E.L. Neil (top), 5 (Simon Warner/bottom), P. Craven 21; Goodness Gracious 25/KeithHarding; Impact Photos John Arthur 34, 40 (bottom)/Alan Blair 8/Julian Calder 40/Piers Cavendish 15/Christopher Cormack 28/Robert Eames 6/David Gallant 10/Tony Page 19 (botttom)/Caroline Penn 37 (bottom)/Simon Shepheard 9 (bottom), 14, 27 (bottom), 33 (top), 38, 39/Bruce Stephens **cover** (bottom left), 4, 9 (top), 32, 33 (bottom)/John Walmsley **title page**/Stewart Weir **contents page**, 11 (right), 12, 13 (top), 17 (both), 18, 19 (top right), 20, 23, 24, 26 (top), 30, 31, 37 (top), 41; Ordnance Survey 7 (top left); Rural Development Commission 13 (bottom), 22 (both), 35 (both), 42; Simon Warner 5 (bottom); Wayland Picture Library 16.

Contents

What is a Village?

A village is a small settlement, surrounded by countryside. Many villages have old buildings, and some may date back to the fifteenth century, such as Ancient House in the village of Clare, in Suffolk. Some villages also have more modern buildings and small housing estates. Compared with cities and towns, which are densely populated, village populations are more spread out and there are more green spaces. Most villages have populations of fewer than 1,000.

Some villages are very small, with only a small cluster of houses around a farm. Others, such as Haxley in Lincolnshire, are larger. Haxley has its own high street shops, church, village hall and schools.

You will often find a village cross in the middle of a village. The cross marks the place where markets and fairs were held in the past. This one is in Meriden, Warwickshire.

VILLAGE POPULATIONS	
Hamlet	10–100
Small village	100–500
Large village	500–2,000

4

During the Industrial Revolution, many people in villages flocked to the growing cities and towns to find work. But today, sprawling railway networks link villages with larger settlements. This allows people who live in villages to work in towns and cities nearby. Now, more and more people are moving away from the hustle and bustle of the cities, to live in the more peaceful villages.

Above Gunnerside is set in the beautiful hills of Swaledale, in North Yorkshire.

Below These scattered houses are found in Uig on the Isle of Skye in Scotland.

5

How villages develop

If you look at a village from above, you can see how it has developed. There are different types of villages. In a 'nuclear village', houses are grouped around a village green or pond. This is where the main buildings can be found, such as the church, school and shops. A 'linear village' has developed along a road and all the buildings are stretched along its length. In the more remote areas of Scotland, crofters' cottages are scattered over the hillsides with their own large plots of land. These are called 'dispersed villages'.

Every village has a reason for being where it is. Natural features such as springs and rivers were ideal locations for early settlements, which needed drinking water. Hilltops provided good defences for some villages. Fertile land was also very important, as villages became centres for farming. Artificial features, such as crossroads, bridges and wells, were also reasons for villages to develop.

The dark hills of this slate quarry tower above the village of Blaenau Ffestiniog, in North Wales.

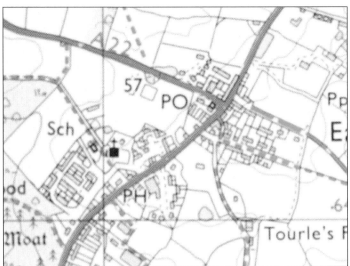

Activity

Use this map of East Hoathly, in East Sussex to find the church (⛪), school (Sch), post office (PO), farms, crossroads and orchard(♤). Then see if you can find them on the aerial photograph.

Above left Maps use symbols to help you identify important landmarks such as a church, school, post office and orchard.
Above This aerial photo of East Hoathly shows the same area as the map.

Sometimes, entire villages were built by wealthy landowners around their grand, country homes. During the Industrial Revolution, some factory owners built 'model villages' for their workers. George Cadbury, the famous chocolate maker, built Bournville, near Birmingham. These model villages were built to a very high standard. Saltaire, near Bradford, had its own church, bath house, library and recreation areas.

In areas of the UK, such as the Welsh valleys, Yorkshire and Ayrshire in Scotland, villages grew up around the coal-mining industry. Houses were built around the collieries for the miners and their families. Sadly, nearly all the collieries have closed down, but the villages are still there today.

People and Communities

Few people in the UK live in villages today. Some people have lived in the same village all their lives, and so did their parents and grandparents before them. For most villagers, the size of the village helps them to feel part of the community. Unlike an inner city, a village has a small population living in one community. In the smallest villages, everyone knows everyone else. In the largest villages, even though people do not always know each other, they still share the same doctor, school and shops.

Only 10 per cent of people in the UK live in villages, but this number is rising as more and more people choose to live in a rural location.

Linton-in-Craven, in North Yorkshire, is a typical village, with a pond and village green where children can play.

Who lives in a village?

Over 200 years ago, most people in the UK lived in villages. They lived and worked in the same area, and rarely travelled. But by the early 1800s, huge numbers of people had moved to the growing industrial towns to work in new factories built during the Industrial Revolution.

Over the past thirty years, the number of village newcomers has risen by 16 per cent. Many of the newcomers work outside the villages in nearby towns and cities. Some people now choose to live in villages when they retire. Villages are also a magnet for wealthy people. This has led to rising house prices in some of the most attractive areas, which is a problem for young people and families. They are unable to find homes they can afford, and are sometimes forced to live in poor-quality housing or to move away from their village altogether.

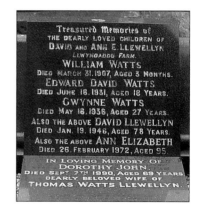

Above Gravestones can show how long a family has lived in the same community. In a village this could be for several generations.

Left Dancing around a maypole is a traditional village activity in some English villages during May Day celebrations.

9

Village homes

Most villages have a mixture of old and new buildings. The oldest houses are often built from local materials. In Devon, many old houses are made from cob (chalk strenghthened with straw) and thatch. Limestone was a favourite building material for homes in the Cotswolds. In Cumbria, you can still see little cottages built from whitewashed stone.

Some big old buildings, such as the Sussex barns and the oast houses in Kent, have now been renovated. Many of the original architectural features remain, but modern facilities such as double glazing and central heating have been added. In popular tourist areas, many beautiful old houses are turned into holiday cottages or luxury homes.

Thatched roofs are made from layers of reeds which are cut and shaped in a traditional way.

Most villages also have small, modern housing estates built on old farmland at the edges of the original settlement. These estates are especially common in villages in which people who work in nearby towns and cities live. The names given to these new developments can provide useful clues about the kinds of features that were there before them, such as Orchard Way, Meadow Lane or Manor Farm Close.

Above Look at the street sign in this picture. Can you guess what used to be on the land where this new housing estate has been built?

Left In Kent and Sussex, oast houses such as this one were used to store hops, used for making beer. Today, many have been converted into homes.

Getting together

Whatever their age, buildings in a village are usually much smaller than in a city or town. The largest buildings are the places where villagers can get together.

The church and its grounds are often the setting for popular events such as a summer fête, or a flower festival, when the whole of the church will be decorated with beautiful flower arrangements. The village hall is usually the main meeting place, used for all kinds of activities. Some remote areas have even been given money from the National Lottery to build or repair their village halls.

Village fêtes are good places to buy delicious local foods such as honey and jam.

Above Many village pubs have gardens, where families can enjoy lunch in the open air.

Public houses (pubs) are also a very important part of village life, where villagers go to relax and chat with their neighbours. They are often linked with traditional sports, as in Somerset, where many are built with their own skittle alleys on the side.

Kentisbeare Village Hall, Devon

Kentisbeare is a small village of 550 people. Plans were first made for a village hall in Kentisbeare in the 1930s, but it wasn't until 1994 that the village hall was finally built.

'It took us six years to raise the money, but we had fun doing it. We had a summer fête with a hot-air balloon, bingo nights and 'safari suppers', where we travelled from house to house, eating dinner in one, pudding in the next and coffee in yet another,' says Queenie Broom, a member of the village hall fundraising committee.

The whole community now uses the hall for a variety of sports. There is also a youth club and a play group, which the village did not have before. The children from the village school even walk to the hall for P.E. lessons, because the school is too small for such activities.

Right The village hall in Kentisbeare, Devon, is used for all kinds of sports, from badminton to aerobics.

A sense of community

Living in a village today is not the same as it used to be. Not everyone is involved in traditional industries such as farming, fishing or mining, which have now declined. Many people commute to work outside the village, or are only able to find a job for part of the year, during the tourist season.

The growing number of people who own cars is also changing the pattern of daily life. Many village people now travel to cities and out-of-town shopping centres for shopping and entertainment. This means that some village shops and village halls have been forced to close.

Well-dressing is a very old tradition. It dates back to the time when wells were blessed to show the importance of fresh water to the village. This dressing is in Hope, Derbyshire.

Even so, there are still many ways in which villagers hold on to their sense of community. Traditions that have lasted for generations help to bring people together. Peak District villages, such as Hope in Derbyshire, still decorate wells with flower pictures at special times of the year. The Miners' Gala celebrations in the pit villages of Nottinghamshire and Yorkshire still attract hundreds of marchers from local villages with their colourful banners.

At this agricultural show, local farmers display their prize farm animals. It is a popular meeting place for local villagers, as well as tourists.

Earning a Living

Since villages are in rural areas, you might think that most jobs are in farming. In fact, only one in fifty people living in villages work on the land today. Villagers have a variety of jobs, and not all of these are based in the village itself. Many villagers have to commute to work by car or public transport to the nearest town or city. They have very similar jobs to people living in towns or cities, and work mainly in the service industries – in shops, offices, banks, schools and hospitals.

75 per cent of land in the UK is used for farming. But only 2 per cent of people in the UK work on the land. Even in remote areas only 10 per cent of people work in farming.

In the past, most people in villages would have worked very close to home on neighbouring farmland. But during the Agricultural Revolution, the invention of fast, new machinery meant there was less work for farmworkers. Also, wealthy landowners took over common land, so ordinary people could no longer grow food there.

Huge farm machinery such as this combine harvester now does the work of many farm workers.

16

Robin Tuppen, Trug-maker

Robin Tuppen has been making trugs and running The Trug Shop in Herstmonceux, East Sussex, for eight years. Trugs are traditional Sussex baskets, made from wood. The Royal Sussex trug is made from chestnut and willow woods, which are carefully shaped and joined together.

'Today, trugs are only made in a few places. We export trugs all over the world. Our workshop employs twelve craftspeople, including Reg Saunders, who has been making trugs for twenty-eight years!' says Robin Tuppen.

Above Some finished trugs.

Left Reg Saunders at work on a trug.

Before large factories were built, whole families worked in cottage industries, making goods such as clothes, shoes and furniture by hand. Other villagers might have worked in one of the nearby country houses of the rich as servants or gardeners. In the small pit villages scattered near large collieries, work in the mines was always close to home.

17

Jonathan Tate, Lime Cross Nursery

Jonathan Tate has always lived in Herstmonceux, East Sussex. Lime Cross Nursery has been in his family for nearly fifty years. Its name is over a hundred years old, and comes from the six very tall lime trees that used to be where the nursery is now situated.

Jonathan explains: *'My parents first used the land as a pig farm and for market gardening. But now I grow conifer trees, which are sold to garden centres across the country. I employ four full-time gardeners.'*

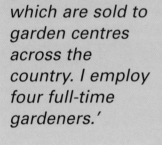

Today, the pattern of farming is completely different from how it used to be. The European Community has made changes in the way land is farmed by 'setting aside' land. This means leaving fields empty instead of growing wheat or grain, which leads to fewer jobs.

Factory farming, where animals are bred indoors in huge sheds, also cuts down on the number of workers needed. Market gardening (growing fruit and vegetables) does employ many people, but the work is seasonal, mainly around harvest time. Fishing still provides employment for some in the fishing villages around the coast of the UK, but competition from abroad has made it difficult for these small village industries to survive.

Left **Jonathan Tate owns a successful Sussex nursery, which provides jobs for some of the local people.**

Tourism is another important village industry, although this is also mainly during the summer months. The main jobs in the tourist industry are in cafés, pubs and restaurants, or in tourist attractions, such as children's farm centres.

Above You might have visited a rural farm centre such as this one. They are popular with families on day trips from the cities and suburbs.

Left Fishing is an important industry in many coastal villages. These fishermen have brought in a good catch.

19

Traditional village crafts are still seen in some rural areas. The craft of building dry-stone walls, a particular feature in the Peak District, is taught by older craftspeople to younger apprentices. The blacksmith's craft still thrives in rural areas where horse riding is a hobby – as horses need to be shod every three months. Saddle-making is another craft that is now being taught to a growing number of apprentices, along with specialist crafts such as thatching.

Working villages

Most villages provide a few local services for the people who live there, but these do not bring many jobs to the area. Since unemployment is growing in rural areas, planners are thinking of new ways to make villages 'working villages', where people both live and work.

Rural business parks such as this one on the edge of Uckfield are made up of small factory units and are bringing jobs back to villages.

Dry-stone walling is a traditional way of building a wall without using cement. Such crafts are still being used to divide farmland in hilly areas.

Rural development projects are trying to help village communities. Planners want to see new workplaces in villages. They are encouraging new businesses, by speeding up the time it takes to get the plans approved. Old, derelict farm buildings are now being renovated and turned into offices and workshops, rather than luxury homes or holiday cottages.

Some new businesses are now choosing to move to rural areas in the countryside as communications improve. It is no longer necessary to be close to a town, or city, for a business to grow and be successful. Businesses can now be set up further from their customers than in the past, and rural business parks are becoming very popular. Large electronics companies and computer manufacturers have chosen rural sites for their businesses.

Activity

Find out from your local library if you have a museum or visitor's centre near you. Collect souvenirs from your visit (tickets, postcards or photographs) and make a scrapbook. If you cannot visit the centre, they may send you some information in the post.

Many villages are trying hard to attract new businesses by setting up special 'telecottage centres', with the help of money from the government. These centres, often in remote areas, give people a chance to learn about information technology. In some coal-mining areas in the UK, the closure of the local colliery has led to very high unemployment. Many ex-miners are now learning how to use computers and run their own businesses at new training centres in rural areas.

Left and below These men are making cheese at the Wensleydale Creamery visitor's centre. The centre has brought new jobs to the area, and provides entertainment for visitors.

Visitor's centres are often opened in a city, town or village for people to see the links between past and present work. The Wensleydale Creamery, near Hawes in the Yorkshire Dales, has opened a visitor's centre, after the closure of the cheese-making factory in 1992. The centre, in the old converted creamery, shows how cheese is made, has a speciality cheese shop and a coffee shop.

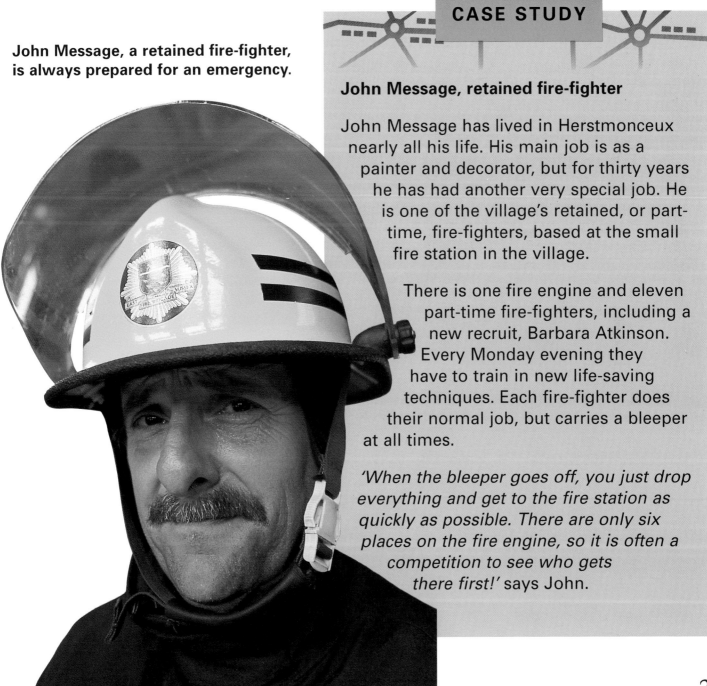

John Message, a retained fire-fighter, is always prepared for an emergency.

CASE STUDY

John Message, retained fire-fighter

John Message has lived in Herstmonceux nearly all his life. His main job is as a painter and decorator, but for thirty years he has had another very special job. He is one of the village's retained, or part-time, fire-fighters, based at the small fire station in the village.

There is one fire engine and eleven part-time fire-fighters, including a new recruit, Barbara Atkinson. Every Monday evening they have to train in new life-saving techniques. Each fire-fighter does their normal job, but carries a bleeper at all times.

'When the bleeper goes off, you just drop everything and get to the fire station as quickly as possible. There are only six places on the fire engine, so it is often a competition to see who gets there first!' says John.

Village Schools

A day in a village school is very similar to that in a city or a suburban school. All schools in the UK have lessons, lunch breaks and playtimes. What is different about village schools is their size.

Village schools are often lucky enough to have large playing fields and green spaces.

A village school usually serves quite a small community, often just the population of the village itself. In remote areas, where the population is very spread out, one school serves several small villages or hamlets. Even so, it is not unusual for a village school to have less than fifty pupils. This is very different from a town or city school, where 500 pupils is quite normal.

Oakwood school, Surrey, was forced to close in 1994 because the number of pupils had dropped too much. This photograph was taken on the last day.

Fewer pupils also means fewer classrooms. A very small village junior school may have only one classroom, with children from as young as five to as old as eleven. Compare this to a typical urban school which has several different classrooms, each containing children who are roughly the same age.

When the number of pupils in a small village school begins to fall, the school may be forced to close. The local council sometimes feels it is too expensive to keep the school running. Local children then have to go to a different school nearby. Villagers often campaign to keep their schools open, because they are worried about longer journeys to school and the loss of a very important community service.

School buildings

No two village schools will look exactly the same. Some are in old buildings located in the heart of a village. They have a long history and are closely linked with village life. They may have been built more than 200 years ago, with money from a wealthy landowner or the local church. Others are in more modern buildings, built by the local council, especially when there have been new housing developments bringing newcomers to the village.

Left **A modern village school.**

Right **Children at Worden Park School in Lancashire sometimes have their lessons outside.**

CASE STUDY

Somerby County Primary School

Laura Stimson is nine years old. She goes to Somerby County Primary School, in Leicestershire. Laura's school was built in 1876 from local ironstone, like a lot of the houses in Somerby.

Laura's school is quite small. There are twenty-six children and three teachers. There are only two classes – one for the infants and one for the juniors. Whenever there's a school trip the whole school goes! In the school, there's a small kitchen and a hall where the children have their lunch and assemblies.

'Mr Weller, our headmaster, says that people from the village have been coming here for generations. You can even see some of their names in the old punishment book!' says Laura.

Some village schools are so small that they have to manage without certain facilities, such as a canteen or a gymnasium. Pupils from a school without these facilities may eat their lunch in the classroom or walk down to the village hall for PE lessons.

Left Laura Stimson likes going to such a small school because it is so friendly.

Below Somerby School's original bell tower blew down in a storm a long time ago, but the old bell is still there.

One of the advantages of a village school is its rural environment. Visits to nature reserves and local beauty spots are often only walking distance away, and there is plenty of wildlife to discover right on the school's doorstep. Grassed areas and lots of open space are also far more common than in built-up areas. The village school in Meppershall, Bedfordshire even has its own open-air swimming pool!

Do you catch the bus to school? In the Scottish islands, some children need to catch a boat!

Getting to school

Going to a village school sometimes means making a difficult journey. For some children, the journey to the nearest school may be too far to walk. Country areas often have few buses, so parents drive their children to school by car instead. Even if the journey is not too far, many children don't walk to school because there are few pavements and cars often drive too fast without looking out for pedestrians. In some of the islands of Scotland, the nearest school is a boat journey away, and bad weather can mean no school for the day!

Activity

Here is a simple plan of a village school and grounds, showing the main buildings and facilities. Try drawing a plan of your school. Ask a friend to help you. You will need graph paper, a pencil, coloured pencils, a ruler and a tape measure.

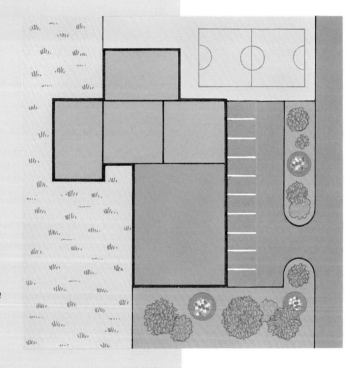

- First, decide which scale to use. Try 1 metre = 1 square.

- Use the tape measure to measure the outer walls of the school buildings, and the boundary of the school grounds. Don't forget to measure the distance from one object to another. Using a pencil and ruler, mark them on the graph paper.

	Field
	Classrooms
	Hall
	Playground
	Garden
	Car park

- In the same way, measure the playground, playing field and car park. Mark them on the graph paper.

- Put in as many features as you can, such as flower borders, benches, trees, and goal posts.

- To measure the length of something that is not straight, measure the object using a piece of string. Then measure the length of string with the tape measure and you will have the correct measurement.

- When you have finished, colour in your drawing and give it a key. Compare your school with the example shown on this page.

On the Move

The rural location of villages makes them less easy to reach than urban settlements. Villages are usually located on small roads several kilometres away from the nearest town, unlike cities which are linked by a network of fast motorways.

In 1973, there were 13.5 million cars on the UK's roads. By 1993, this number had risen to 20.1 million.

Being far away from the hustle and bustle of city life makes villages popular with tourists who are looking for a peaceful, rural environment. For the people who actually live there, having to travel long distances for shops, entertainment and other important services doesn't always seem so good!

This cycle track was once a busy railway line.

In the morning and evening rush-hours, village stations are busy with trains and commuters, but are almost deserted in the middle of the day.

Growing villages

About 200 years ago, villages were largely cut off from the outside world, but the 'Railway Age' changed this for good. In 1826, work began on the world's first passenger line, from Liverpool to Manchester. By the 1880s, nearly 32,000 km of railway track linked towns and villages all over the UK.

By the 1920s and 1930s, railway networks had snaked out all over the countryside. This meant that people could still keep their jobs in the cities but live in the peace and quiet of the countryside. Some people lived in new housing estates, built around the villages at the edges of cities. As the cities grew, these villages were swallowed up and became part of the cities' suburbs.

Commuter villages further out in the countryside, especially near big cities, have also grown as large housing developments are built near the main railway lines into cities.

In many villages there are few bus services. Some have no bus at all because it is no longer profitable for bus companies to operate in rural areas. Some local councils help to pay for private buses or provide special bus services themselves. Some village railway stations have also closed down or have been turned into pubs or tea shops.

This village bus in Craigiau, Wales takes villagers into the town of Cardiff to do their shopping.

Villages and cars

In villages today, cars are the main means of transport. The huge increase in cars during the last thirty years means that villages now have to cope with more traffic than they were originally designed for. On busy roads, fast-moving cars are a danger to pedestrians. One solution is traffic calming, where coloured road surfaces encourage drivers to lower their speed.

Activity

In Belfast in Northern Ireland, most facilities are within 2 km of the city centre. But in the village of Carnlough, villagers have to travel to Ballymena, 22.5 km away, to find a shopping centre. The nearest hospital is in Antrim, about 48 km away!

Compare the distances people have to travel using a village and a town near you. From your local library, find an Ordnance Survey map showing a village and a town plan in a road atlas. From the centre of each settlement, use the scale to work out how far it is to the nearest hospital, supermarket and leisure centre. Note the distances in a table.

Post buses can deliver people as well as letters!

Post Buses, Staffordshire

In Staffordshire, post buses have been introduced in remote areas. They are used to provide transport for local people as well as for collecting and delivering mail. The post buses are very popular with older people. Some post buses even have specially fitted ramps for people in wheelchairs. They are also ideal for tourists, who can leave their cars at home.

Some villagers feel angry about the extra pollution caused by so many cars. Some village high streets can become so congested with parked cars that local councils have to build car parks especially for visitors. Country wildlife and old buildings can also be badly affected by car fumes.

Even so, about 75 per cent of villagers have their own cars to travel outside the village. This can have a bad effect on village life, as money spent outside a village may lead to local shops and services closing down. Services in the nearest town are likely to be several kilometres away. If there are no trains or buses, villagers without cars have problems doing simple things. Seeing the doctor or doing the shopping become difficult without transport.

Special coloured stripes on some roads remind drivers to slow down as they go through a village.

Shopping and Entertainment

Many of the shopping and entertainment facilities found in a town or city, such as supermarkets, theatres, cinemas and sports centres, are not found in a village. This seems hard to imagine if you live in a built-up area, where even the local high street has a number of different banks, shops and take-away restaurants!

If a village is lucky enough to have its own village shop, it will be a busy place, combining many different services in a small building. People meet in the shop to exchange news, as well as to do their shopping. There may be a post office section, general store area and perhaps even a video hire section. Some shops may also sell local crafts, which are popular with tourists.

In a survey by the Rural Development Commission of nearly 8,000 villages, 43 per cent had no post office, 29 per cent had no village hall, 40 per cent had no permanent shop and 90 per cent had no bank.

This is the main shopping street in Burford, Oxfordshire.

Some village shops have always been happy to deliver groceries to the homes of villagers after they have done their shopping. But now, to survive the competition from out-of-town superstores, they are doing much more. Many village shops now have fax machines, photocopiers and even a computer for villagers to use.

Long Preston Post Office, North Yorkshire

Long Preston Post Office shop in Yorkshire is a really important part of the community. The shop uses every centimetre of space, and stocks over 3,000 different types of groceries! The shop also sells wine, beer and newspapers. The photocopying, fax and word-processing services are very popular, along with dry cleaning and photo-developing. As there is not a chemist in the village, the shop is also a 'pick-up-point' for prescriptions from the local doctors.

Above The shelves stock everything from bread to batteries!

Above Long Preston Post Office is more than just a place to buy stamps.

Mobile services

In some villages, a mobile library visits every week, on its route visiting remote villages all over the area. If a village does not have a permanent shop, a mobile shop visits once or twice a week. In Dorset, a converted bus travels around the county's villages, giving young people the chance to take part in clubs and projects.

Meeting places

The main meeting place for entertainment in a village is usually the village hall, pub or at local church events, such as fêtes. The village green or recreation ground is another place where many outdoor activities take place. Traditional games, such as cricket, are also part of village life in some villages. Tug-of-War is often popular at village fêtes.

Activity

Make a survey of what people do in their spare time where you live. List different options and then ask your parents, friends, relations and teachers. The questions could look like this:

What do you do in your spare time?
- ❏ Go to the cinema?
- ❏ Go swimming?
- ❏ Go to a restaurant?
- ❏ Read?
- ❏ Play football or cricket?
- ❏ Go on country walks?

Present your information on a bar chart like the one on this page to show which activity is the most popular.

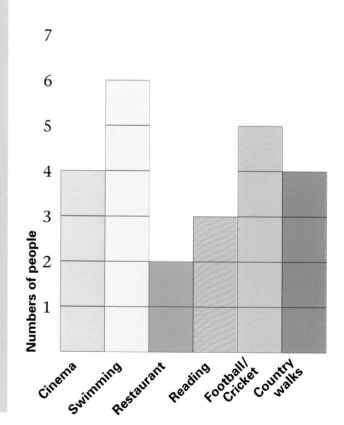

Even so, many young people feel there is not enough for them to do in a village. Sports facilities may be a few kilometres away, and without transport, these are difficult to visit. To help solve this problem, the people of Penryn, Cornwall, have set up a special centre for young people, where they can enjoy abseiling, climbing and sailing.

Above **Children enjoying their newly-built adventure playground.**

Enjoying the countryside

Walking, rambling and cycling are popular ways to spend leisure time. All over the UK, projects have been launched to encourage more cycling in rural areas. Cycle paths have been laid alongside the routes of disused canals and railway tracks. This network of paths can also be used by wheelchair users and parents with pushchairs.

Below **Many people visit the countryside to enjoy long walks in a peaceful, unspoilt environment.**

The changing use of the countryside attracts more people to rural areas. Golf courses, riding stables and rural visitors' centres have opened up.

Change and the Future

Villages are attractive places to live in, with beautiful scenery and a peaceful environment. Even so, villages do need to change and think of the future. Some villagers are quite happy with the way things are, and are worried that changes will harm their peaceful way of life. Others, particularly older people and young families without transport, often find living in a village quite lonely. There has to be a balance between keeping the good things about village life and making changes to improve it. Planners need to look at new developments very carefully to make sure villages can continue to thrive without losing their character.

Nature can reflect the changing industries in rural areas. In Yorkshire, around the coal-mining areas, one type of moth camouflaged itself over the years. Its wings gradually went black so it could hide amongst the trees and hedges, which were black with coal dust. In recent years, with the decline of the coal industry, the moths are now gradually returning to their original white colour.

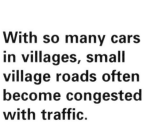

With so many cars in villages, small village roads often become congested with traffic.

Pleasley Vale Business Park, Derbyshire

This vast old textile mill built in Victorian times during the Industrial Revolution has now got a new lease of life! The building has been converted into workspaces, bringing new businesses to the area. There are three main buildings for factory use, and at the entrance gates, two lodge buildings are being converted into offices. The companies that already rent the workspaces include a textile designer and a boat builder.

When the building was a textile mill, ventilation was very important because of all the textile fibres in the air, so there are hundreds of huge windows. New companies say they love the feeling of space this gives to the new conversions.

More jobs

Over the last fifty years, because of the lack of jobs, many villagers have gradually been forced to travel to work in nearby towns. Now, with the help of government money, many new rural business centres are bringing jobs back to rural areas. In Shropshire, a new project called 'Wheels 2 Work' lends mopeds to teenagers. They can then ride to work. This is very useful when public transport is not running.

Pleasley Vale Business Park, which was once derelict and vandalized, has now got a new lease of life.

Creating jobs is important in villages, but we also need to protect the environment. In one Scottish village in the Highlands, cutting peat to use as fuel for the new whisky distillery would have created jobs. But the plans did not go ahead because the land would have been damaged.

To make sure that people continue to spend money in villages, villagers are encouraged to buy local produce, which is grown on nearby land.

It is also important to stop local businesses from closing down. Some villagers buy shares in a local shop or pub to keep it in business.

Peat cutting in Scotland. Finding new jobs in village areas is important for the local economy, but should this be at the cost of the environment?

Tourism brings new jobs to villages. Tourists use village stations, and spend money in tea shops and country pubs.

Parish councils are now becoming more interested in the opinions of young people living in villages. The councils want to elect more young people, as they feel this is the only way they will really understand what young people need. Village communities are now looking to the future and are really working hard to improve village life.

Activity

Would you like to improve something in your area? Perhaps you and your friends could carry out a survey of ideas to improve your school environment. You could ask questions similar to those below, or make up your own.

● Are you happy with the school environment as it is?

● Would you like more play equipment, such as an adventure trail?

● Would you like a conservation area, with wild flowers to attract butterflies and insects?

● Is there enough space to play football, or would you like a special area for ball games?

When you have collected your data, display the information in a table. If you have access to a computer, you could print your results using computer graphics.

Some villages are lucky enough to have a Youth Centre.

How to Investigate a Village

There are many ways to start investigating a village. Here are some ideas for you to consider.

First-hand information

The village post office is a good place to start. Look at the notice board for local events and advertisements for jobs and services. Local newspapers include news about daily village life. The letters page will show you what people think about changes and future plans for the area. Some television programmes also have features on village life.

People in the know

Parents, teachers, relatives and neighbours are likely to have visited or lived in villages. Try talking to them about their experiences.

Your local library can provide all kinds of information about villages. The reference section is particularly useful. The librarian will help you to find census information, Ordnance Survey maps, books, encyclopaedias, magazines and newspapers.

The local parish council or the planning department of the nearest county council can send you information about future plans for the area, along with facts and figures. They may also have a special Education Officer, who can help you with this kind of research. The nearest County Record Office will have old papers and maps that you can use to find out how an area has changed over the years.

Maps

A road atlas will show you where a village is in the UK, but you will need a larger-scale map to see it in detail. Try looking at village street plans, which are sometimes shown in a map book covering a whole county. Each plan will show you all the local roads, green areas, important buildings and landmarks. An Ordnance Survey map will give you all this in much more detail.

Census information

Census information shows how areas have changed over the years, and what they are like now. The information includes the numbers of people living in an area, their ages, whether or not they are single, married or divorced, where they were born, whether they are working, unemployed or retired, what kind of housing they live in and whether or not they own a car. You can find census information from a large public library.

Places to visit

Museums, farm centres, rural visitors' centres, nature reserves, and tourist information offices.

Collecting and presenting your evidence

Collect all the information you can find – leaflets, bus or train tickets, museum guides, postcards, newspaper cuttings – and design your own village scrap book or poster promoting the area. Try using other types of media, such as CD-rom encyclopaedias, photographs or tape recordings of interviews. Also, if you have access to a computer, you could try entering your findings on a database.

Notes About this Book

The main text in each book in the Landmarks series provides general information about four types of settlement within the contexts of communities, work, schools, transport, shopping and entertainment, and change. Each book in the series features the same areas of study so that the four different types of settlements can be compared easily with each other within a general context.

Case studies give specific information about a particular aspect of each chapter and often provide direct quotes from people who live and work in different kinds of settlements. Children can use this information to make a direct comparison with their own experience.

The activities are designed so that children from any type of settlement can do them. They can be used to demonstrate what the main text has already stated about the locality mentioned in the book, or as a contrast. Throughout the series children are encouraged to work with the various tools that a geographer uses to study a particular area, such as mapping and graph skills, conducting surveys and using primary source evidence such as census material.

Introduction (pages 4–7)
This chapter gives a brief outline of the different types of villages found in the UK. The language and examples have been designed to encourage children to look around them, and either compare or contrast their own settlement with that of a village. The text examines what features make villages rural localities, why some villages are situated in specific locations and how they differ from each other.

Activity on page 7:
This activity is designed to illustrate how you can compare an aerial photograph with an Ordnance Survey map. The children are invited to identify objects and features shown on the map using a simple key, and then to see whether they can find the same features on the aerial photograph. This activity introduces children to the idea of using a key. Ordnance Survey produce a variety of maps, including large scale maps down to 1:10,000 scale.

People and Communities (pages 8–15)
Because village settlements are small, they have traditionally been places where there is a strong 'sense of community'. Children are encouraged to think about what this means, by looking at the kinds of people living in a village, its key buildings and focal points of village life. In what ways do the children's experiences differ?

Earning a Living (pages 16–23)
This chapter deals with the village economy, what kinds of jobs people do and how the type of work found in villages has changed in recent years. Children are encouraged to think about land use and how the nature of a settlement influences the types of employment found there. Encourage the children to think of their own locality and what types of employment exist there. How does their experience compare with the examples in the text?

Activity on page 22:
This activity is designed to show children how jobs are linked with their locality and how they can find evidence of this. Follow-up work could include asking them to compile a brief report of their visit, including any of the artefacts they have collected, or perhaps putting up a class display.

Village Schools (pages 24–29)
This chapter focuses on children's experiences, by encouraging them to compare or contrast their school and its surrounding neighbourhood with village examples illustrated in the text. How many children are there in their classes? Are all the children in their class the same age?

Activity on page 29:
This is a simple mapping activity aimed at encouraging children to think about size, proportion and the purpose of using a key on maps to differentiate between different types of land use.

On the Move (pages 30–33)
This chapter encourages children to think about the importance of good communication links between settlements. Children should be asked to think about how they get to school, the effect of cars on the environment and the benefits of public transport.

Activity on page 32:
The purpose of this activity is to show the distances from villages to key services. This emphasizes the isolation of many villages. Children can produce a table of distances from two contrasting settlements (a village and a town are just suggestions) to various facilities. This information can then be used to produce a bar graph so the two settlements can be compared visually.

Shopping and Entertainment (pages 34–37)
This chapter shows how the character of a village is reflected in the local shops and facilities, and how these are changing.

Activity on page 36:
This activity encourages children to take into account differing opinions by conducting a survey. This skill can then provide them with data which can be translated visually into a bar graph, or even a pie chart. Why are some activities more popular than others?

Change and the Future: (pages 38–41)
This chapter shows that whilst rural localities are attractive places to live, the changing way of life can bring problems, which need to be resolved.

Activity on page 41:
This activity encourages children to think of questions to assess their peers' opinions. The information gathered from the survey can be input into a spread sheet using a computer.

How to Investigate a Village (pages 42–43)
This section is by no means a definitive guide, but it does provide some useful ideas on where to find information about villages for project work or classroom discussions.

Glossary

Aerial Viewed from an aeroplane.

Agricultural Revolution A period during the eighteenth century, when the development of new farm machinery and land laws led to fewer jobs on the land.

Apprentices People who learn trades or crafts under the direction of skilled workers.

Census A survey of the UK population carried out once every ten years.

Collieries Coal mines and all their buildings.

Congested To become blocked up.

Declined When something has become worse.

Densely populated When an area has a lot of people living in it.

Exports Goods that are sold abroad.

Industrial Revolution A period of time during the eighteenth and nineteenth centuries, when the development of new machinery led to the growth of factories in the UK.

May Day A traditional holiday at the beginning of May, when workers get together to celebrate.

Mobile Moving from place to place.

Nature reserves Areas of countryside where wildlife is protected.

Parish councils A group of local people chosen to manage a number of village communities.

Permanent Something that is always there.

Planners People who make plans about the development of an area, usually working for a local council.

Profitable Money-making.

Remote Far away.

Renovated Repaired and improved.

Rural In the countryside.

Urban Built-up areas.

Venues Locations at which people can meet.

Books To Read

Investigating Maps by Selma Montford, (Young Library Limited, 1993)
Mapwork 2 by Julie Warne and Mandy Suhr, (Wayland, 1992)
Settlements by David Flint, (Heinemann, 1993)
Settlements by Nick Millea, (Wayland, 1992)
The United Kingdom by Christa Stadtler, (Wayland, 1991)
The United Kingdom by David Flint, (Simon and Schuster, 1992)
United Kingdom by Peter Evans, (BBC Educational Publishing, 1996)
Where I Live – Commuter Village by Neil Thomson, (Watts Books, 1993)

This map shows villages in the UK mentioned in this book.

Index